Social Media Addiction

The Ultimate Guide for Finally Overcoming This Time-Consuming Addiction

Copyright 2015 by Caesar Lincoln - All rights reserved.

This document is geared towards providing exact and reliable information in regards to the topic and issue covered. The publication is sold with the idea that the publisher is not required to render accounting, officially permitted, or otherwise, qualified services. If advice is necessary, legal or professional, a practiced individual in the profession should be ordered.

In no way is it legal to reproduce, duplicate, or transmit any part of this document in either electronic means or in printed format. Recording of this publication is strictly prohibited and any storage of this document is not allowed unless with written permission from the publisher. All rights reserved.

The information provided herein is stated to be truthful and consistent, in that any liability, in terms of inattention or otherwise, by any usage or abuse of any policies, processes, or directions contained within is the solitary and utter responsibility of the recipient reader. Under no circumstances will any legal responsibility or blame be held against the publisher for any reparation, damages, or monetary loss due to the information herein, either directly or indirectly.

The information herein is offered for informational purposes solely, and is universal as so. The presentation of the information is without contract or any type of guarantee assurance.

The trademarks that are used are without any consent, and the publication of the trademark is without permission or backing by the trademark owner. All trademarks and brands within this book are for clarifying purposes only and are the owned by the owners themselves, not affiliated with this document.

Table Of Contents

Introduction

Chapter 1: How Social Media Has Changed Our Lives

Chapter 2: Am I Really Addicted to Social Media?

Chapter 3: Good and Bad Effects of Social Media

Chapter 4: How to Handle A Social Media Addiction

Conclusion

Introduction

First off, I really want to thank you for downloading this book. The pages in this book were developed through years of experiences that I have gone through, as well as what has proven to work for others that I have talked to and have researched. I also want to congratulate you for taking the time to understand your own social media addiction and how you can overcome it.

After experiencing issues with social media addiction and struggling to overcome them, I decided that I wanted to write a short, detailed book to help other people who are in a similar situation as I was. I also wanted to help people understand how social media addictions can be detrimental to our overall health and self-esteem. Many people have relatives or friends who struggle with social media addictions and the people around them are not able to understand what is going on in their heads.

I can guarantee that you will find this book useful if you make sure to implement what you learn in the following pages. The important thing is that you IMPLEMENT what you learn. Addictions are not conquered overnight but the important thing to remember is that it is definitely possible for you to overcome them. What I am giving you is the information needed so that you can understand your own dependent relationship with social media as well as the steps needed to make that journey.

Many people experience social media addictions in their lives, as it is becoming more and more necessary to be connected in today's world. A certain amount of social media use can help us to take advantage of amazing technology but past a certain point, it becomes a leech that sucks the energy and time out of our day. As you go through these pages, you'll get a better understanding of what social media addiction really is, the signs of it, and you will learn several ways that you can overcome it. We will also dive into what work is required of you to get past the roadblocks you have.

I recommend that you take notes while you are reading this short ebook. This will ensure that you get the most out of the information in here. I want you to feel that you made a purchase that is worth your money and I want you to look over the notes of this book even after you've finished reading it. The notes will help you to pinpoint exactly what you need to implement and by writing things down, you will be able to recall specifics and how to handle certain situations when they arise.

Lastly, remember that everything in this book has been compiled through research, my own experiences, as well as the experiences of others, so feel free to question what you have read in this book. I encourage you to do your own research on the things that you want to look deeper into. The more you understand about your own mind and body, the better off you'll be. To overcome a social media addiction in your life, it will take some work on your part but you can do it! So remember to read with confidence and an open mind!

Chapter 1:

How Social Media Has Changed Our Lives

The Unthinkable

Accidentally cut off all connections to your friend? Looking for someone you haven't seen in years? Trying to find out the name of that stranger you met today? These things were difficult, even impossible, to accomplish before the era of the Internet. Ever since the Internet presented its wonders to us, it has become easier for us to communicate and connect with people around the world.

With just a few clicks, you can now search for someone you haven't seen in years. With just a few clicks, an idea that used to take days to deliver can now be conveyed in a matter of seconds.

This is how the Internet era has changed the way we communicate. Access to the Internet has changed our lives, and it is continuing to change us even more as new social media services are being created every month.

The Age of Social Media

Social media is a form of electronic communication through which people build online communities for the purpose of sharing information, personal messages, ideas, and other content such as images, documents, and videos.

If there was ever a period in time when social media reached its peak, it is today. We can no longer get by without using any variation of social media. Popular variations include social networking sites such as Facebook and Twitter, blogging sites such as Tumblr, media sharing sites such as Instagram and YouTube, and many others.

We must provide these variations for simplification purposes, for social media is a wide and general category. To simplify things further, examples in this book will focus on the four most popular social media websites today: Facebook, Twitter, Tumblr and Instagram.

The use of social media is even making it's way to children in middle schools and high schools throughout the world. These kids are especially susceptible to becoming addicted to social media websites, mainly because they are at a time in their lives where they are searching for meaning and other people to relate to. Another reason is because of the free time they have. Many adults have busier schedules so they aren't as free to use the Internet for long extended periods of time. Many children, however, have many hours a day of free time and can use them how they choose.

Chapter 2:

Am I Really Addicted to Social Media?

How do you know if you are really addicted to social media? Have you ever wondered what your reason for using social media all the time is? Is it just for fun, or is it something more? Provided here are the ten most common symptoms of social media addiction.

How to know if you are addicted to social media

You feel that personal and bugging responsibility to check any, if not all, of your social media accounts at every possible free moment. This is the most obvious sign of addiction. From the moment you wake up, you feel the urgent need to check your account(s). You feel the need to check your mobile phone or laptop when you are eating or out and about with friends.

You spend most of your time on the Internet. This is another common symptom of social media addiction. You delay your other tasks just so you can spend your time on Facebook, Twitter, Tumblr and other social networking websites. You can spend hours on the Internet but you can't manage to keep yourself focused on some other task for even an hour. Much more than that, you lose track of time whenever you are online. Your 30-minute break becomes a two-hour break.

You are experiencing the "Did someone like my post?" syndrome. You make it a point to check your accounts to see if someone has liked or commented on your post – may it be a status message on Facebook, tweet on Twitter, or photo on Instagram.

You have this personal obligation to take a picture of almost everything and post it to your accounts; from your food, your pet dog, your new clothes, the book you're reading at the moment – you feel the need to post these photos somewhere.

You share everything about anything. May it be a funny conversation among strangers that you overheard or a funny conversation between you and your friends or family, you immediately think of posting it on Facebook or tweeting about it.

You go out of your way just to make sure you have access to your accounts anywhere you go. The most common example of this is: you look for Wi-Fi signal everywhere.

You mourn over your loss of Internet access. You feel bored whenever you are not spending your time online, and you can't manage to stay put without the Internet.

What's happening online is becoming a huge part of your life offline. When people are buzzing over a certain issue online, you feel that you must also be part of it even when you're not involved and you feel greatly affected by what's happening online.

You use Internet expressions in daily conversations. This is one of the biggest signs that you've been spending too much time on the Internet. Expressions include saying "LOL (Laugh Out Loud)" or "IDK (I don't know)" even when talking with your friends in real life. Because you use these expressions so much when you are on social media, you tend to include these in your daily vocabulary.

You want to get involved in almost everything in your social media accounts. Being unable to do so results in the uncomfortable feeling of being left out. When you haven't checked your account for two days or so, you feel that you've missed out on something big.

Do these symptoms sound familiar? Imagine that this list of symptoms is a checklist. How many have you checked? How many are you experiencing? If you have checked at least two to three things, then you are still on the normal track. However, if you are experiencing most or all of these symptoms, then it is definitely serious and something should be done.

Chapter 3:

Good and Bad Effects of Social Media

Let's face it: social media is already becoming a necessity. Anything can have good and bad effects on people, especially if this thing is being used in excess. Social media is not an exception. What then, are the good and bad effects of social media?

Good effects of social media

Social media enables its users to have easier communication with people – may it be their friends, family, colleagues or acquaintances. Social networking websites make it simple. With just a simple tweet or message on Facebook, you can tell anyone from anywhere, anything. It does not matter if the person is living in another country, because the message will reach them. Also, most people use their social media accounts more than their actual phones, so social media becomes an effective (and cheap) way to convey a message.

You get to expand your network when you are part of social networking sites. You can meet people from all walks of life with the same or different interests. This is good for business people since it is advantageous for them to have an expanded and wide network. It is also beneficial if you have an interest that is not very popular in your local community. It allows you to connect with those who have common interests all around the globe.

You get to be updated about certain issues. When something big happens, like a hurricane or large sporting event, it spreads rapidly across the Internet. The term for this is "going viral". If browsing through your social media accounts is already a hobby, then it will only take you a few minutes to stumble upon news articles about the latest issues shared by your friends, and immediately, you'll get yourself updated on the latest happenings.

Social media increases efficiency because things can be done at a greater speed. Virtual meetings, discussions and transactions can be done using social media. Nowadays, most transactions are happening online already. This lessens the hassle of manual transactions and it saves people a lot of time.

It is undeniably true that social media is the outlet of many people to voice out their thoughts on a certain issue or to simply discuss matters. Since people of different cultures and different beliefs meet up on social networking websites, an in-depth discussion on issues can be expected. Social media, especially blogging, can be used by people as their platform to be able to put into words their opinions on things. Blogging is therapeutic for most people because it enables them to clear their minds of both their good or disturbing thoughts.

The Internet is a perfect example of a place where anyone can participate and speak up. There are no boundaries when it comes to freedom of expression online. However, it must be taken into consideration that you must be responsible for what you say online and must always respect other people's opinions.

Social media is one of an advertiser's greatest tools. Since a lot of people are spending most of their time on the Internet, a company that is advertising their products has some sort of assurance that their advertisements will reach a large audience.

You learn from the people you interact with online. This may be because you are both part of a discussion, or you've read their posts concerning their opinions on certain things. Either way, you get to learn from other people's opinions. Also, when you are learning on the Internet, you do not only have to hear from a single perspective. People will always have a say regardless of if it is with or against your perspectives, and if taken the right way, this will surely allow you to understand other perspectives better.

They say that anything taken in excess is bad for you, and this applies to social media as well. Now that we've gone through the good effects of social media, it is time for us to take a look at the bad effects of social media. While reading, take some time to pause and to think about if you may be experiencing the same effects in your own life.

Bad effects of social media

Social media lessens productivity for most people. This is probably the worst effect of social media for the majority. It does increase efficiency if it is being used for the right purposes; otherwise, people tend to become unproductive because of spending too much time on the Internet. You might have experienced delaying your tasks because you are too absorbed in what is happening on your accounts.

Among students and even employed people, social media prevents them from finishing their work early. Instead of being able to finish something ahead of time so you could do your other tasks, you are unable to do so because of the time you wasted on the Internet. Procrastination on the internet is even more prevalent with students these days because they can even use the internet on their phones while sitting in class! It is almost like the people who are on social media on their phones in a public place are actually not even present mentally, only physically.

Social media causes personality changes in some people. Because some people have become so addicted to social media, their social relationships with other people have changed. Because of spending too much time online, there is the tendency of having less interaction with one's family and friends. The worst part of this is that it is usually not noticeable until things get bad. You may physically interact with your family or friends a little less each day, until you are only having a short 5-minute conversation with them because you want to get back to the computer.

Also, one of the worst effects of social media is that it tends to develop self-esteem problems in people, especially teenagers. Cyber bullying is common among school-age teenagers and when done at an extreme level, it yields very negative results. People tend to take other peoples' comments and posts negatively and they start to have doubts about themselves. They tend to lose confidence in themselves when criticized.

Not only is cyber bullying a problem, but pretty much every social media platform uses ratings such as "likes" or "thumbs up" to show the reception of other people. This may help some people to feel confident about themselves if they receive a lot of "likes" on something about them.

However, many people compare the "likes" they receive to other peoples' amount of "likes". This is an endless cycle because nobody in the world is liked by everyone and basing your self worth on others' opinions of you is the recipe for unhappiness.

Too much time on social media platforms can actually be dangerous. When you share everything about anything, you tend to allow people to invade your privacy, especially when you share personal matters online. Hacking is a serious problem and having your personal information like bank accounts and passwords exposed on your social media accounts is very dangerous and risky.

When you are on the Internet almost all the time, you tend to feel that you actually "belong" to the virtual world. You make friends, you foster friendships and sometimes you even establish a name and reputation on the Internet. However, there are times when these friendships and fame do not trickle down to real life. This type of situation may cause people to feel socially awkward in real life, thinking that they do not belong in the said society because they do not have, and are not experiencing, the same friendships and fame that are present on the Internet.

A common bad effect of social media is its effect to one's health. Whether you admit it or not, you have delayed your sleep sometime in your life just so you can spend more time online. However, there are some people who do this every day and this is definitely detrimental to your health. People are not only losing sleep but sometimes they even starve themselves because they feel that they are not hungry when in fact they are skipping meals and lose their appetite while sitting and browsing.

Looking at these bad effects of social media, we can say that at some tipping point, social media becomes unhealthy. If while reading this book, you've felt that you've experienced these bad effects sometime in your life, then it may serve as motivation for you to step up and make a big change. Do not wait for the worst case scenario to happen to you before you decide to change your habits.

Chapter 4:

How to Handle A Social Media Addiction

The purpose of this book is to try to help you overcome your addiction to social media. It must, of course, begin with you. Once you've assessed yourself and you are not denying that you are indeed addicted to social media, you can start helping yourself.

How to get out of a social media addiction

Accept the fact that you are indeed addicted to social media. Denying that you are addicted to social media will delay the recovery process. With the numerous warning signs and symptoms shown in the previous chapters, there are clear guidelines for you to compare to your behavior.

Go out and explore the outside world. Even if you are one of those people who has already become awkward in socializing with people in real life, you must try your best. Keep your determination intact. After all, you used to socialize with other people before you got addicted to the Internet. You just need to go back to these old habits.

Participate in your old hobbies. Do the things you used to do, like reading books, listening to music, or playing sports. Once you go back to these old interests, slowly you'll find yourself losing interest in social media and you'll realize the huge gap that social media has incurred. You can never fully enjoy yourself while sitting in front of a computer for hours and just looking at pictures and videos and talking to people on the Internet. Life outside the Internet is always so much better.

Manage your time. Prioritize your tasks and create a strict schedule for yourself. Using social media is fine as long as it is necessary to complete your tasks, but otherwise, make it your last priority. Discipline yourself in such a way that you plan out everything that you need to do; you follow your schedule with minimum distractions and without fail. Once you are done with all important tasks, then you can spend some time on the Internet again.

This time, you can do so without interruption since you've already completed your important tasks. Make sure to have an end time for your social media use as well. If you want to complete all of your important tasks for the day by 9 o'clock and use social media after that, make sure to put a cap on the time you are allowed to use it or else you will stay up late and revert back to the old habits that you had.

Find another outlet for your emotions. After all, people started with journals before blogging websites came into the picture. With this, you can avoid getting into arguments and debates with certain people over your controversial opinions. Although arguments and debates widens one's perspective and deepens discussion on the topic, sometimes it's not worth it, especially if these arguments will only waste your time and energy. If this is the root of the problem, then it's better to stay away from trouble than to approach it on purpose.

If you really can't control your impulse to check your accounts at every possible time, it is highly suggested that you ask your best friend or the one you trust the most to change your account passwords and keep them from you. This lessens the distraction brought about by social media because there is no way that you can access your accounts.

This is very effective when you need to complete an important task, yet you cannot focus because you are distracted. Another strategy that is similar to this is to block the website(s) that you are addicted to and ask a person you trust to make up the password so that you can not access the sites even if you are desperate.

If you feel that social media is not doing you any good (i.e. health and personality problems), then the best thing for you to do is to delete your accounts. If all else fails, you must cut off the source of the problem before you can begin treating your social media addiction. This way, no matter how strong and how often you feel the urge to check your online accounts, you can no longer do so because they've been deleted.

Also, once your accounts are gone, you can now focus on living your life normally and try restoring your relationships with people – just like before you got addicted to social media. With this strategy it is important to note that you will feel a strong urge, for the first few days or even weeks, to check your social media accounts to see what new updates you have. You must ride out these urges and find something else to do in these situations. As each urge passes, you will notice that you will find it easier and easier to find joy in the real world activities again.

The tips and suggestions provided in this chapter are only useful if you put them into practice. They are very easy to say, but the actions are much more difficult. This is why the challenge for you is to follow these tips if you really want to change yourself. You cannot get out of your social media addiction by simply staring at these plain words – there is no one who can help you, except yourself.

Remember, there is no finite time that we can use the Internet. There is always one more thing we can do on social media. We can leave one more comment, look at one more picture, or watch one more video. But when you feel yourself getting drawn in to using your accounts more than you need to, a good question to ask yourself is "In five, ten, fifteen years from now, will I be happy that I spent my time doing this or is there something I can do right now that my future self will be proud of?" If you can think of something your future self will be proud of, shut off the browser and get started.

Self-Discipline Is The Key

It's difficult not to be addicted to social media given its wonders and the ease and convenience that it provides. Roaming around the Internet is like living in a different world, you can see odd and amazing things with just a few clicks. The Internet is like the fantasy that you can never live in, which is also what makes it a wonderful place to be part of. However, we are always forced to come back to reality and deal with our problems no matter how long we postpone them.

In order to balance things out, the challenge for you is to instill self-discipline in yourself. Without self-discipline, nothing can be done about your problem. Learn how to prioritize and manage your time. Eventually, you'll see for yourself that social media, when used wisely, is definitely one of the biggest benefits to mankind.

Conclusion

I worked hard on creating the best guide for "overcoming a social media addiction" that I could. Social media addiction was stopping me from accomplishing many things in my life. After finally overcoming my issues, I wanted to give back to others. These are all the strategies and information that have worked for me, as well as others that I have talked to and researched. I guarantee if you stay consistent they will work for you as well. Be optimistic about your current situation and make small progress each day!

If you feel like you learned something from this book, please take the time to share your thoughts with me by sending me a message. I would really appreciate it! You can also leave a review on Amazon if you'd like.

Thank you and good luck in your journey!

Printed in Great Britain
by Amazon